Evangelistic

A CHRISTIAN'S POCKET GUIDE

TO

'This small booklet is something you should not be without if you want to be effective in your evangelism among Muslim people. A very useful tool, giving you Knowledge, help and encouragement.'

Dr. Elsie A. Maxwell

Evangelistic
                V
A CHRISTIAN'S POCKET GUIDE
TO

MALCOLM STEER

CHRISTIAN
FOCUS

Scripture quotations are from The Holy Bible, English Standard Version, copyright © 2001 by Crossway Bibles, a division of Good News Publishers. Used by permission. All rights reserved.

ISBN 978-1-85792-915-7

© Copyright Malcolm Steer 2003

First Printed in 1997
Published in 2003,
reprinted in 2004, 2008 and 2015
by
Christian Focus Publications, Ltd.
Geanies House, Fearn, Tain,
Ross-shire, IV20 1TW, Great Britain.
www.christianfocus.com

Cover Design by Daniel Van Straaten

Printed and bound by
Nørhaven, Denmark

All rights reserved. No part of this publication may be reproduced, stored in a retrieval system, or transmitted, in any form, by any means, electronic, mechanical, photocopying, recording or otherwise without the prior permission of the publisher or a licence permitting restricted copying. In the U.K. such licences are issued by the Copyright Licensing Agency, Saffron House, 6-10 Kirby Street, London, EC1 8TS www.cla.co.uk.

CONTENTS

Introduction 7

1. Islamic Beliefs and Practices 9

2. Misunderstandings about the Gospel 27

3. Arguments against the Gospel 39

4. Getting the Message Across 49

5. Getting the Approach Right 57

Appendix 75

INTRODUCTION

This book is a companion booklet to 'A Christian's Pocket Guide to Islam' and its purpose is to provide some help in witnessing to Muslims.

Effective witnessing depends on:

1) Getting to Grips with Islam – that is, having some knowledge of the beliefs and practices of Islam, including the nature of Islam and being aware of some of the crucial differences between Islam and Christianity (Chapter 1).

2) Getting the Message Across – that is, being aware of some of the misunderstandings that Muslims have about Christianity, being aware also of some of the arguments used by Muslims against the Gospel and then knowing how to positively present the good news of Christ (Chapters 2–4).

3) Getting the Approach Right – that is, knowing how best to approach a Muslim and then knowing what to do and say (Chapter 5).

This is the general outline and direction of the book. For further reading please refer to the appendix.

The material used in this booklet, subject to some revision, was originally printed in *Light on Islam*, published by UCCF in 1981 and 1988 (second edition), and then reprinted by FFM (Fellowship of Faith for the Muslims) in 1997 as 'A Pocket Guide to Christian Witness to Muslims'. Much of the material in chapter 5 was originally written by Bryan Knell, founding coordinator of (CRIB) Christian Responses to Islam in Britain.

CHAPTER 1

ISLAMIC BELIEFS AND PRACTICES

In this chapter as well as considering basic Islamic beliefs and practices we also want to take a brief look at how Islam developed.

1) The Rise of Islam

The pre-Islamic age in Arabia is known as the 'Times of Ignorance' with the population composed of scattered nomadic tribes and the majority being pagans. One of Arabia's pagan shrines, the Ka'aba at Mecca, was the scene of an annual pilgrimage. The pagans were polytheists believing in one Supreme God and many lesser deities. Also on the Arabian peninsula were scattered groups of Jews and Christians.

Muhammad was born in Mecca in AD570. Little is known of his early life, except that he was orphaned when very young and brought up by his grandfather and then an uncle. He was very religious, took to fasting and meditation, and often had vivid dreams. As a result of his marriage at the age of 25 to a wealthy 40-year-old widow named Khadijah for whom he was working as a caravan manager, he became a person of importance. Because of his wife's wealth he no longer had to work and had more time for meditation. Dissatisfied with the polytheism and crude superstitions in Mecca, he became convinced of the supremacy of the one God. He was almost certainly influenced in his beliefs by contact with Jews and Christians. At the age of 40 he received his first revelation and thereafter claimed to be a prophet of God.

He encountered opposition and was forced to flee Mecca in AD622 and went to Medina. The flight to Medina, called the 'Hijra', is considered to be 'year one' in the Islamic calendar. At Medina he became a religious and political leader, believing that he was called of God to re-establish the true principles of a religion which had become corrupt. Later the new religion spread throughout the Arabian peninsula. At the time of his death, in AD632, he had succeeded in creating a religious force which encompassed the economic, cultural and political structure of everyday life. Within ten years of his death, Islam had spread throughout the Middle East, and within a century it reached across North Africa, into Europe, across Asia to China and down into India.

2) The Nature of Islam

It is essential to understand two important concepts concerning the nature of Islam. Firstly, Muhammad taught, and his followers believe today, that Islam is not only the true religion but a religion that was not new when Muhammad proclaimed it. Rather, it represents the message which had been given to all the prophets from Adam onwards, i.e. the religion of 'submission' (the meaning of the Arabic word 'Islam') – submission not so much to God as a person but to the revealed will of the one true God. The revelation of God's will has been granted through a long succession of prophets. In that sequence of prophets which includes Abraham, David and Jesus, the last prophet is Muhammad. Islam then both contains and supersedes what has gone before.

Secondly, Islam is far more than just being a religion – it is a total and unified way of life, both religious and secular. It provides guidance for all walks of life – individual and social, material and moral, economic and political, legal and cultural, national and international. Consequently, religion and politics are the two sides of a single coin in Islam.

3) Development within Islam

It is important to consider at least two developments within Islam.

I) Division into Sunni and Shi'ite sects.
Of the many divisions that developed within Islam the largest division is between the Sunni and Shi'ite branches.

The basic cause for this division was a difference of opinion as to who should succeed Muhammad. The Shi'ites are a minority group who, although they accept the first three 'caliphs' (successor) as true leaders, believe that the true line continues through Ali, who was Muhammad's son-in-law. They also differ over their interpretation of the Qur'an, and tend to be less democratic than the Sunnis, often ascribing divine power to their leaders – a characteristic which has been shown concerning the Ayatollah Khomeini and his successors in Iran where the Shi'ites are in the majority.

II) Sufism. In stressing the transcendence of Allah, Islam's orthodox teaching failed to satisfy the desire for personal religious experience. The Sufis are those within both Sunni and Shi'ite Islam who sought, in their direct experience with God, to fill this gap – the need for human experience. The Sufis are known as the mystics of Islam.

4) Beliefs and Practices of Islam

The religion of Islam consists of two parts: Belief ('Iman') and Practice ('Din').

I. Belief – All Muslims are required to believe in the following six fundamental articles of faith:

a) One God (Allah) – Muslims lay tremendous emphasis on the unity, majesty, transcendence and sovereignty of the one true God. He has no partner or children. According to Islamic doctrine the power and immutability of Allah make him the author of all things, whether they seem good or bad to us.

b) Angels – There is a hierarchy of angels who are reasoning created beings. A leading angel is Gabriel who transmitted the Qur'an to Muhammad. Two recording angels attend every person, one to record his sins and one to record his good deeds. There are also spirits called 'jinn' which were created from fire. They may be beneficent but are usually evil. The Devil is said to be the father of the 'jinn'.

c) Holy Books – Muslims are taught that Scriptures have been given to many previous generations through their prophets. The total number of these sacred books is believed to be 104 of which the first 100 have been lost. Of the remaining four, one each was given to Moses – the Pentateuch ('Torah'), one to David – the Psalms ('Zabur'), one to Jesus – the Gospel ('Injil') and one to Muhammad – the Qur'an.

The Qur'an, a book about the same length as the New Testament, has 114 chapters (Suras) which are not normally arranged in chronological order. It is said to have been revealed to Muhammad during the last 23 years of his life and to have existed eternally in heaven in its present form and language (Arabic). Muslims believe that the Qur'an corrects and abrogates previous Scriptures because it was revealed last. Furthermore, Muslims assert that the books of the prophets (Old Testament and the Gospels) have been changed and that they are no longer useful, except where they happen to be in agreement with the Qur'an.

Second only to the Qur'an as a source of Islamic law and life are the traditions called in Arabic the 'Hadith'. These are records of what Muhammad did, said or approved of. As such they form a model for conduct and a basis for law.

d) Prophets – According to the traditions there are 124,000 prophets in number. In the Qur'an the names of 28 prophets are found, most of whom are biblical characters. There are six Great Prophets: Adam, Noah, Abraham, Moses, Jesus and Muhammad. Though the Qur'an refers to the sins of the prophets (with the exception of Jesus), Muslims generally believe that all of God's prophets were sinless. The Qur'an refers to the virgin birth of Jesus, his miracles and calls him the 'Messiah', the 'Word of God' and the 'Spirit of God'. But it states that Jesus was not the Son of God and that like other prophets he only had a human nature and was created by God. Furthermore, Muslims believe that he was not crucified but called into heaven while someone else (perhaps Judas) was made to look like Jesus and crucified by mistake in his place.

e) Day of Judgment – On the Last Day, all humanity will be raised again to life and judged according to their deeds. Each person will be examined from their own book of deeds which will have all their words and actions recorded. All deeds and words will be weighed in a balance scale – one balance being over paradise and the other over hell. The righteous will enter paradise where material gifts will be lavished on them and they will enjoy many physical pleasures.

f) Predestination – This means that Allah has decreed (predetermined) all things, good or evil, from eternity. Everything is subject to his unchangeable decrees.

II. Practice – These doctrines are accompanied by the five pillars of Islam which are practical duties that every Muslim must perform.

a) Recitation of the Word of Witness ('shahada'). The confession of faith 'There is no God but Allah and Muhammad is the Apostle of Allah' is to be repeated frequently. A person also becomes a Muslim by the recitation of this creed.

b) Prayer – Muslims are called to ritual prayer five times a day. After completing the ceremonial washing they face Mecca, and follow prescribed gestures while repeating prescribed prayers in Arabic.

c) Fasting – The fast is obligatory during the whole month of Ramadan (the ninth month of the Muslim lunar year), the time changes each year according to the lunar calendar. The fast, which includes abstinence from smoking and marital relations, is from first dawn to sunset.

d) Almsgiving – There is an obligatory payment on different kinds of property and income known as the legal alms ('zakat'). It should be distinguished from voluntary alms which are given over and above this.

e) Pilgrimage ('hajj') – Every Muslim who is physically and financially capable of doing so is required to make a pilgrimage to the House of God (Ka'aba) at

Mecca once in their lifetime. There are numerous rites attached to this pilgrimage.

It is worth mentioning that some Muslims regard 'Jihad' as a sixth pillar of Islam. The word means 'exertion' (on behalf of God) and is often interpreted to mean Holy War.

5) Islam and Salvation

In the light of the above beliefs and practices it is important to consider the teaching of Islam about salvation and their understanding of God, humanity, sin and forgiveness. Although what is presented here in brief is the orthodox position, some Muslims may disagree with this view especially as there has been a tendency in recent years to use concepts more acceptable to Western thinking. In chapter four a response will be given to the points made here.

So exaggerated is the emphasis on the transcendence of **God**, that he is portrayed as a being who is so utterly remote and self-sufficient that he cannot be known, neither can he be affected in any way by his creatures. This emphasis on the absolute transcendence of God and on his absolute sovereignty leads to an exclusion of any moral quality, for it reduces all God's attributes to his will and power. Love, mercy, holiness and wrath are mentioned in the Qur'an as attributes of God, yet because of his absolute transcendence they are to be understood only as mere expressions of his will with no motive. God cannot be limited and bound by any pervading law of morality. He is free and can exercise his power in whatever way he wishes.

Humanity is God's creation and its primary duty is submission to the will of God as revealed in the Qur'an. Original sin is denied, for human beings are born without a sinful nature. Their nature before and after the Fall is unchanged. However it is thought that human beings are created weak and become sinners through personal wrong deeds.

Sin, to the Muslim, is either a saying which blasphemes God or an act which breaks the Muslim rules of prohibition. There is no concept of humanity being in a state of sinfulness, but simply that each sin is just one act in a series of acts or sins. Sin does not grieve God, who is too great to be affected. Thus there is no concept of a divine hatred of sin. Sin only breaks a law, not a fellowship such as between a son and his father.

Good deeds balanced against evil deeds on the judgment day may help gain **forgiveness**, but in reality God forgives whom he wills and punishes whom he wills. There is no need for God to base his forgiveness on a moral foundation. Thus the Muslim sees no need for a Saviour and there is no way of salvation other than by works. If the Muslim was asked, 'What must I do to be saved?' the answer would be, 'Believe in God and his apostle Muhammad, and do what God requires, and if God so wills he will accept you.' There is therefore no assurance of salvation in Islam.

Thus Islam fails to diagnose humanity's condition as sinful, unable to know and obey God perfectly, as well as failing to reveal God in his true holiness and self-giving love for sinful humanity. It also fails to provide a Saviour from sin and death and fails to give the sinner assurance of forgiveness and peace with God.

Insofar as a person can influence their eternal destiny at all in Islam, a person's own efforts are their only source of hope.

CHAPTER 2

MISUNDERSTANDINGS ABOUT THE GOSPEL

There is usually no lack of opportunity to speak about our faith with Muslims. In most cases your Muslim friend will want to talk about what they believe and will ask questions about Christianity. However, we all know what it is to be misunderstood. Although we might use the same words and expressions, they convey different meanings to different people. Some might even reject the use of certain words and expressions because their understanding of what they mean is not only different from ours but contrary to their own belief system.

This is particularly true of the way Muslims have understood certain concepts of Christianity. From its very inception Islam formed a misunderstanding of these concepts and over the centuries further misunderstandings have developed. This means that if we want to get our message across, we need to be aware of the misunderstandings and seek to remove them so that Muslims will have an accurate picture of what Christians really believe.

There are basically five misunderstandings and these are:

1) that Christians believe in three gods and that the Trinity is composed of God, Mary and Jesus.

The subject of the Trinity should not usually be raised when talking to a Muslim about the Christian faith but if they ask about it the subject should not be avoided. The oneness of God must be emphasised, as well as showing that any discussion on the Trinity has nothing to do with the number of gods, but with the nature of God. It must also be emphasised that Mary is not part of the Godhead, but that the Bible shows this one God revealing himself as Father, as Son and as Spirit or –

perhaps in an easier way for the Muslim to understand – you may say that God reveals himself as Creator, Word and Spirit. This does not mean that God changed himself from one thing to another, for he always existed in these three ways.

Of course, God is a mystery far above our thought and no Christian can explain exactly how God exists in three ways. Neither will a Muslim claim to explain the nature of God. If the Trinity is nothing but a metaphysical puzzle, as some Muslims contend, what about the orthodox Muslim doctrine of the Unity of God, which is defined in terms of the relation of God's eternal attributes to each other and to God's eternal essence? Is that not also a metaphysical puzzle? The doctrine of the Trinity is simply the way the Christian tries to summarise what the Bible teaches about God, Jesus and the Holy Spirit. Rightly understood, this doctrine exists to **defend** the unity of God.

2) that the expression 'Son of God' used of Christ refers to a merely carnal relationship in which God took a wife and produced a son.

Obviously it should be explained that this expression does not refer to the physical coming of Christ, but to the eternal relationship that Jesus had with God who is called 'Father'. Mary was simply the human agent by which Jesus was introduced into the world. We can give illustrations to show that when the expression 'son of something' is used in everyday speech it conveys a spiritual meaning like a metaphor and does not imply physical sonship. Examples: 'son of the road', 'son of a leopard', 'sons of thunder'. Emphasise, then, that we speak of the Son of God only in a spiritual sense.

However, even if this is understood, the basic problem is knowing how to overcome the Muslim belief that Jesus was a created being who does not eternally exist. A popular Muslim title for Jesus found in the Qur'an is the expression 'the word of God' and if this is linked with the Muslim's belief concerning the nature of the Qur'an it provides a bridge for communicating both the pre-existence and deity of Christ.

Both Christians and Muslims agree that God is eternal and that God's Word is eternal. The eternity of God and his Word are one and the same thing, for God is one. Moreover, both Muslims and Christians agree that God bridges the gulf between the infinite and finite by revealing this eternal Word to his finite creation. For Muslims, God expresses his eternal Word within the created world through the book called the Qur'an. Hence, most Muslims call the Qur'an the eternal Word of God. For Christians, God expresses his eternal Word within the created world through a person called Jesus. Hence, the Bible speaks about the eternal Word of God becoming flesh, the man Jesus (John 1:1-3, 14).

This matter of God speaking to humanity through his Word can be illustrated by human speech. Where was my word before it came out of my mouth? In my brain and in my thoughts; but if you cut open my head can you find my word there? In some mysterious way I and my word are the same and cannot be separated. Whatever my word does, it is I who am doing it. How could Jesus have authority to forgive sins (Mark 2:1-12) or be judge on the Last Day (Matt. 25:31-33)? This is only possible because Jesus is the Word of God. What he does is the action of God himself.

However, avoid saying that 'Jesus is God' as this will be inevitably misunderstood and gives the impression that we make Jesus into another God besides God. This is not what we mean. Rather, we mean that God's eternal Word came to have a human life among people as Jesus Christ, i.e. Saviour and Messiah. The New Testament emphasises that God sent Jesus (John 17:3, Rom. 3:25, 5:8, 2 Cor. 5:19) and that the work of Jesus is entirely for the glory of God (John 12:27, 28). Therefore, let us witness with this emphasis on what God did in Christ and on faith in God through Christ.

3) that the death of Christ would have been an unworthy ending to his life and is not necessary to provide forgiveness of sins.

Muslims reject the doctrine of Jesus' atonement for sins. They reject it firstly on historical grounds. If Jesus survived the cross, as the Muslim believes, then he could not have given his life to atone.

Secondly, the Muslim idea of God and his decrees recognises no need for atonement. Islam emphasises the absolute freedom of God. He does whatever he wills and so if God wants to forgive he simply forgives.

Thirdly, humanity does not need an atoning sacrifice. The popular belief is that good works (such as prayer, fasting and almsgiving) can 'atone' for a person's sins. Even if these good works are not enough, 'God is merciful' and so the Muslim hopes that in the Last Day God may overlook his failings.

Now our Muslim friend must firstly understand that any fair reading of the New Testament shows that the death and the resurrection of Christ are central to the New Testament message. Major portions of the Gospel accounts are dedicated to these events. Jesus himself continually predicts these events and in fact reprimands his disciples for failing to understand that as the Messiah he must suffer, die and rise from the dead. Jesus saw himself as the fulfilment of many Old Testament prophecies relating to his suffering and death. He determined to sacrifice himself out of love for humanity and in obedience to God. So that, although it is true that the people of his day opposed Jesus and plotted to kill him, yet Jesus in accordance with the will of God voluntarily laid down his life. God approved the sacrifice that Jesus made by raising him from the dead.

It is important to explain the meaning of Christ's death. Firstly, it puts an end to all other sacrifices. A study of the sacrifices of the Old Testament is most effective in showing that the people approached God by the way of sacrifice. The sacrifice of Jesus cleanses our guilt and brings us into fellowship with God (Heb. 10:11-25).

Secondly, Christ's death assures us of our forgiveness. Of course this cleansing from guilt is not automatic. It needs to be accepted by faith through trusting in the One who died for our sins. We need to emphasise that the way of salvation

is not a matter of first trying to be righteous in order to make ourselves worthy
of salvation, but rather first coming as
an unworthy sinner and accepting God's
free forgiveness as a gift.

Thirdly, Christ's death reveals the hor-
ror of sin and the righteousness of God.
Sin deserves to be judged and punished.
But God in his mercy allowed the suffering and judgment to be carried by Jesus
the Saviour. Through Christ crucified
God offers us forgiveness, but also shows
us his righteousness (Rom. 3:21-26).

4) that Christianity is a Western religion.

It is argued that as its followers are main-
ly found in Western countries, termed
Christian countries, all the inhabitants
are Christian and as these countries represent Christianity so their actions reveal
what Christianity is really like. As we
have already observed, Islam is for the
Muslim a total system having important
national, social and political implications
and it is very easy for the Muslim to
regard Christianity in the same way. In
seeking to remove this misunderstanding

we need to deal with both the origin and the true essence of the Christian message.

As far as the origin of Christianity is concerned we can point out that as Jesus Christ was born in Palestine, it is here that the origin of Christianity is to be found. Palestine is the land that joins the three great continents of Asia, Africa and Europe and it was from here, using the famous Roman roads and trade routes, that the Christian message was able to spread rapidly in all directions. Today Christianity is growing rapidly in many non-Western countries.

We must also point out that the true essence of Christianity is spiritual and primarily concerns our relationship with God. Although the Christian message should affect us in a total way yet it is, by nature, very different from the total system of Islam. Furthermore, it is important to point out that although Christianity is not individualistic yet it demands an individual response. There is no way in which we can Christianise society. The Church as a community is an essential element of the Christian message but no-one is naturally born into that community. Therefore we make a clear distinction between nominal and real Christianity.

5) that the Bible is not reliable, having been changed or corrupted from its original form.

The Qur'an frequently refers to the holy books of the Jews and Christians and calls such people the 'People of the Book'. Muslims view the Qur'an and Islam as a continuation and fulfilment of previous revelations and therefore regard all previous prophets and holy books as proclaiming essentially the same message as the Qur'an. However, it is obvious to all that great differences exist and Muslims believe that the differences have been caused by changes and corruptions introduced by Christians and Jews into the Bible during the course of history. Muslims frequently assert that such claims are made on the basis of the Qur'an. They also assert, on the basis of the Qur'an, that the Scriptures previous to the Qur'an have been abrogated by the Qur'an.

However, in actual fact the Qur'an does not teach that the previous Scriptures given to Jews and Christians are textually unreliable or have been abrogated. The Qur'an supports the existence, availability, integrity and universal significance of these Scriptures. It enjoins belief in these Scriptures upon all and even claims that the Qur'an confirms them (Sura 5:43-52, 70-72). In fact, if Muhammad himself is in doubt, the Qur'an tells him to appeal to Jews and Christians and to their Scriptures (Sura 10:95).

A multitude of ancient manuscripts of the Bible in its original languages and in translations – manuscripts long antedating the era of Islam – abundantly testify to the preservation and integrity of the biblical text. The Muslim is unable to produce an 'unaltered' Bible and give evidence of the so-called corruptions and changes. Even if a group of unbelievers had desired to make changes to the Bible after the time of Muhammad, it would have been an impossible task in view of the number of copies of Greek and

Hebrew Scriptures available and the way that these had been scattered throughout the world. Total suppression of these Greek and Hebrew Scriptures would have been impossible.

Another charge commonly heard is that the Christian Gospel is not the original Gospel given through Jesus. Muslims claim that Jesus took the 'Injil' (the Gospel) into heaven at the time of his ascension and that since the Christians have four Gospels they cannot be the original Gospel. At best the four Gospel accounts now available are unreliable Christian traditions, at times even contradictory. Furthermore, the Muslim considers that since our Gospel records are mostly narrative, they are inferior to the Qur'an, for they regard the direct speech of God as the highest form of inspiration and the stories of Jesus a secondary form of inspiration. Now, as we have already observed, the Qur'an does not state that the 'Injil' is textually unreliable and neither does it say that the original Gospel was taken into heaven.

On the subject of the number of Gospels we can point out that according to the

Bible there is only one Gospel, the Gospel of Jesus the Messiah. He himself is the Gospel. The four Gospel accounts in the Bible are four accounts of one and the same Gospel. Thus the account by Mark is really the Gospel of Jesus the Messiah according to Mark ('The beginning of the Gospel of Jesus Christ...' Mark 1:1).

F.F.Bruce writes, 'At a very early date it appears that the four Gospels were united in one collection. They must have been brought together very soon after the writing of the Gospel according to John. This fourfold collection was known as 'The Gospel' in the singular, not 'The Gospels' in the plural...About A.D. 115 Ignatius, Bishop of Antioch, refers to 'The Gospel' as an authoritative writing...' (*The New Testament Documents: Are they reliable?*, IVP, 1960 – page 23). Furthermore, there is abundant evidence to show that it is perfectly reasonable to accept the four Gospel records as historically reliable and authentic.

Often the impression is given by Muslim writers that there were hundreds of other accounts of the life of Christ that were systematically destroyed after the Council of Nicea. (See Chapter 3 concerning 'Gospel of Barnabas'.) But it must be pointed out that no single Council was responsible for arbitrarily collecting and proclaiming a list of books as canonical. Rather, the New Testament books became authoritative because the Church regarded them as divinely inspired with apostolic authority (whether direct or indirect). The first ecclesiastical councils to classify the canonical books did not impose something new upon the Christian community but rather codified what was already the general practice of those communities. (See F.F. Bruce, ibid, Chapter 3 – 'The Canon of the New Testament'.)

In actual fact this matter of the integrity of the Bible is not a problem for the majority of Muslims, and generally they are quite willing to read the Scriptures, especially the Gospel records, and accept them as authentic documents. It is important for us to realise, though, that there is a unique difference between the nature and purpose of the Qur'an and the Bible. For this reason it should not be our intention to engage in a 'battle of the books'. The real issue is between the Qur'an and Christ, not the Qur'an and the Bible. The purpose of the Scriptures is to lead us to Christ. There is no salvation in the Scriptures themselves, neither do we 'worship' them. Jesus said, 'You search the Scriptures, because you think that in them you have eternal life; and it is they that bear witness about me, yet you refuse to come to me that you may have life' (John 5:39-40). We, therefore, pray that as Muslims read the Scriptures they might be led to Christ the Saviour.

CHAPTER 3

ARGUMENTS AGAINST THE GOSPEL

Islam stands and falls by the statement that Muhammad is the last prophet who brought the final revelation from God to humanity. So that in addition to a rejection of the doctrines of the Trinity, Atonement and Deity of Christ, serious attempts have always been made to try and convince Christians that they should accept Muhammad. One way that this has been done is to argue against the Gospel by either trying to show: 1) that the Gospel of Barnabas is the only authentic reliable Gospel or 2) that our Scriptures contain prophecies concerning the coming of Muhammad or 3) that the message of Jesus was for the people of Israel only. Therefore, before continuing our discussion about communicating the Gospel, we ought to take a brief look at these three points.

1) The Gospel of Barnabas: is it authentic?

Muslims claim that the Gospel of Barnabas is the only known surviving Gospel written by a disciple of Jesus and that it was accepted as a canonical Gospel up until the Council of Nicea in AD325. From that time, it is argued, the Christian Church has ignored and suppressed it. It was supposed to have been rediscovered by a Christian monk called Fra Marino who came across an Italian manuscript in the Pope's private library in 1590. He smuggled it out of the library, read it and became a Muslim.

In fact the only known existing text of the Gospel of Barnabas is in Italian in the Vienna Library. This text, dated in the sixteenth century, was edited and translated into English by Laura and Lonsdale Ragg and published in Italian and in English in 1907. Since then Muslims have translated this work into Arabic, Urdu and other languages. In the

1907 publication the introduction gave internal and external evidence to show that the Gospel was a medieval forgery but this introduction has been omitted from all Muslim publications.

The Gospel of Barnabas incorporates a number of normal Muslim allegations: Jesus is not the Son of God; Judas Iscariot, not Jesus, dies on the cross; Jesus prophesies the coming of Muhammad, etc. It contains most of the events found in the four Gospels but with many things artfully turned to favour Islam.

Now if we refer to ancient manuscripts of the New Testament dating back to pre-Islamic times and to which the Qur'an refers and testifies to their truth, we find no record of a Gospel attributed to Barnabas. Neither is there any mention of it in the list of the books which constitute the Bible by the Church fathers. Furthermore, according to the New Testament, Barnabas was not one of the twelve disciples of Jesus and was not even named Barnabas until after the ascension of Christ (Acts 4:36). All external and internal evidence indicates that the Gospel of Barnabas is a forgery of European origin, dating from about the fourteenth century or later.

The author, a Christian who embraced Islam, simply utilises materials from the biblical Gospel accounts, omitting and altering at will to suit his purposes. But apart from this and other geographical and historical errors, one example from this work will indicate that he not only contradicts the Gospel but also the Qur'an. In many places 'Barnabas' makes Jesus declare that he is not the Messiah, but that Muhammad will be the Messiah. This statement contradicts both the Gospel and the Qur'an since in both books Jesus alone is the Messiah.

Fortunately, not all Muslims accept the Gospel of Barnabas as a genuine Gospel account. In fact one Muslim scholar has said, 'In the light of the Christian rejection (of the Gospel of Barnabas as a genuine gospel) the contention that this work is genuine can be validated only when a copy of it that antedates the mission of the Prophet has been discovered and brought to light – which thus far has not been possible' (quoted in 'The Gospel of Barnabas: An Essay and Inquiry' by S Abdul-Ahad and WHT Gairdner. Henry Martyn Institute of Islamic Studies, India, 1975).

2) Is Muhammad foretold in the Bible?

There are a number of Qur'anic passages that encourage Muslims to seek for predictions of Muhammad in the Bible. So on the basis of these passages Muslims have searched exhaustively through the Old and New Testaments for proof that these two books indeed contain prophecies of the coming of Muhammad. Of course, they soon realise that the Bible prophecies refer to the coming of Jesus and the coming of the Holy Spirit and not Muhammad.

However, Muslims still believe that the coming of Muhammad was foretold and particularly appeal to two portions of the Bible to substantiate their claim, i.e. Deuteronomy 18:15, 18 and John 14–16.

With the first passage the Muslim contention is that the prophet was to be raised up, not from the people of Israel but from among their brethren. They argue that Ishmael, father of the Arabs, was a brother of Isaac and that the phrase 'from among your brethren' clearly refers to the Arabs and to Muhammad as the Arab prophet.

In answer to this it is an undeniable fact that Jews are much more truly brothers to each other than to Arabs, as history has shown. Furthermore, the word 'brethren' most naturally refers to the people of Israel (cf Deut. 17:14, 15; Lev. 25:46). Even if we accept the correctness of the Muslim interpretation of 'brother' here, why should Ishmael be selected rather than some other close relative of Abraham or even of Isaac or Jacob, such as, for example, Jacob's brother Esau, from whom the people of Edom are descended?

Muslim interpretation of this passage pays no heed to the biblical evidence which refers to its fulfilment. Jesus said, 'If you believed Moses, you would believe me, for he wrote of me' (John 5:46), inferring that the prophecy of Moses relates to Jesus himself as the prophet to come. Acts 3:17-26 and 7:37 clearly understand

Jesus to be the fulfilment of the Deuteronomy verses.

In the John passages under considera-
tion, Muslims claim that the Greek word
paracletos which is translated 'helper' should
read *periklutos* or 'praised one', which would
have the same meaning as Ahmad or Muhammad. However, no sound evidence in
the New Testament manuscripts supports
this Muslim assertion. Even if Muhammad
is the 'Paraclete' (Helper) as some Muslims
have said, it is obvious from all that is said
about the Helper that it can only refer to the
Holy Spirit. This is clearly stated anyway
in 14:26. None of these passages from John's
Gospel suggest that the disciples were to
wait some five centuries before the fulfilment of his promise. In Acts 1:5 we read
that the time of the Spirit's coming was
very short. It was subsequently fulfilled
just ten days after Jesus' ascension on the
day of Pentecost.

3) Was Jesus a national prophet to Israel only?

In order to secure the universality of
Muhammad as the seal of all prophets,

Muslims have tried their best to deny Christ's universal claim (John 14:6). The best way of achieving this has been to demote him to the last national prophet of Israel. Thus, he loses all significance for the Gentiles to whom Muhammad claims to be sent. Statements such as 'I was sent only to the lost sheep of the house of Israel' (Matt. 15:24) and Matthew 10:5-6 are used to support this claim.

There are, of course, passages in the Bible that do speak of his universal ministry, for example, Jesus said 'I am the light of the world' (John 8:12). There are passages in the Old Testament concerning the Servant of the Lord and his universal mission, passages which, according to the New Testament, find their fulfilment in Jesus (compare Isa. 42:1 with Matt. 12:15-21). However, Christians gladly agree with Muslims that Jesus, while he was on earth, to a large extent limited his ministry to the people of Israel. The reason for this goes back to Genesis 12:2-4 where we read that through the seed of Abraham all the nations of the earth will be blessed. So Jesus confesses to the Samaritan woman at the well (John 4) that 'salvation is from the Jews' (note: not 'to the Jews').

Only the Jews could understand the significance of Christ, for he was embedded in the history and the inspired writings of Israel. The Jews were waiting for him. He had to be a Jew (Deut. 18:15) and he had to be a descendant of Judah and the house of David (Gen. 49:10, 2 Sam. 7:13). Every Jew expected the Messiah, even though they did not recognise him at his coming.

So only the Jews – and only after they had understood him – could proclaim him to others; hence all the apostles were Jews. Jesus, after his resurrection, clearly explained to his disciples that this message of 'repentance and forgiveness of sins should be proclaimed in his name to all nations, beginning from Jerusalem' (Luke 24:47). Therefore Jesus in the Great Commission ordered his disciples to 'make disciples of all nations' (Matt. 28:19, 20), and even though it took a while for the apostles to understand this, eventually they began to carry out this command.

An illustration (adapted from *Mission to Islam and Beyond* by Jens Christensen) might help our understanding. In many countries, without an irrigation system, the fields have no water. Therefore the water is channelled and localised by means of canals, viaducts, tunnels and channels until it reaches the fields where it is then allowed to flow out freely. Now concerning the water of life we can say that the channels for the life-bringing water were the Jews and that the apostles were the final sluice gates which brought the water to the fields that represent the world.

It is therefore consistent that in his lifetime Christ prepared the channels that would bring the water to the fields. Even his help to the Gentiles, such as the Roman centurion, served as a lesson for his own disciples. He said, 'Truly, I tell you, with no one in Israel have I found such faith. I tell you, many will come from east and west and recline at table with Abraham, Isaac and Jacob in the kingdom of heaven, while the sons of the kingdom (Jews) will be thrown into the outer darkness ...' (Matt. 8:10-12).

CHAPTER 4

GETTING THE MESSAGE ACROSS

In this chapter we want to mention a number of specific areas of need that we can concentrate on in Christian witness. We make a great mistake if we assume that all Muslims are theologically minded. The majority are not. Rather, they have the same needs as the rest of us, and in presenting the Gospel we are seeking to meet 'the hunger of the heart'.

This chapter is, therefore, basically a response to the section in chapter one on 'Islam and Salvation'. Having also now understood the need to be aware of various misunderstandings as outlined in chapter two, we can positively share the Gospel along the following lines:

1) Knowledge of God: explaining the concept of revelation and how the one true God reveals himself through Christ.

Many Muslims are sincerely seeking after God. The God of Islam is often perceived as being so great and powerful that he becomes remote and impersonal. Religion is simply a tightly defined legalistic system rather than a relationship of love between God as Creator and human beings as the created. Many Muslims try to satisfy the desire for personal religious experience through Sufism. We can share how the one true personal God who loves humanity and who desires a relationship with human beings has revealed himself to us in a personal way through Christ, so that we might come to know him as our heavenly Father.

2) Forgiveness of sins: explaining the concept of atonement and how the one true God forgives us through Christ's sacrifice.

Both Islam and Christianity call on people to repent, but such a call depends on the concept of sin, that is, on what one is called to repent from. Muslims believe they are sinners because of some evil which they have committed, and not because of original sin or the nature of their hearts. Therefore, in Islam the call is to repent from infringements of the ritual and moral code and to seek to wipe out small sins by good deeds.

We need to explain carefully the biblical concept of sin and show that the forgiveness we need is more than the cancellation of bad debts in a great book of accounts. It is of the utmost importance to relate to Muslims that, like everybody else, they are rebels against God, because of their very thoughts, speech, work and life. Everyone, therefore, needs forgiveness in order that a right relationship between God and the individual can be established. For sin separates us from God and it is only on the basis of Christ's sacrifice that we can experience true forgiveness and be brought into fellowship with God. In actual fact many a Muslim is plagued by guilt feelings over wrongs committed and is sincerely seeking for assurance of forgiveness.

3) Assurance of salvation: distinguishing between law and grace as the basis of acceptance before God.

Both Islam and Christianity teach that God forgives sin, but the basis of forgiveness is different. In Islam, salvation rests upon one's own shoulders and obedience to the law, while in Christianity it rests purely and solely upon the grace of God. Islam tells a person what they must do to earn salvation; Christianity tells a person what God has done to give them salvation. In Islam there is therefore no assurance of salvation, for in this world Muslims cannot know for certain whether God has destined them for paradise or hell. As a response we can share that, although we do not consider ourselves to deserve God's forgiveness, yet on the basis of the cross, God offers us salvation to be received as a gift by faith. Emphasise that good works are important in Christian living, but our salvation is not dependent upon these works.

4) Change of heart: distinguishing between outward reform and inward change.

In many Islamic countries a determined effort is under way, by the Islamic leaders, to bring their society more in line with the principles, laws and regulations of Islam. Sometimes such actions bring the religious hierarchy into conflict with certain sections of the population, who react and rebel against a new Islamic fundamentalism that seems so negative and restrictive.

It also illustrates the teaching of Christ (Mark 7:14-23), where we learn that what defiles human beings is the corrupt heart, which cannot be changed by mere outward reform. People are unable to make a new character for themselves. They cannot make an evil desire become good or change a love for sin into a love for righteousness. We can share, therefore, that only new life and power from God can change a person and give that person the capacity to live a life of righteousness in obedience to the will of God.

What we are saying, then, is that we need to emphasise what is unique in the Gospel of Christ. Dr William Miller (who spent over 40 years as a missionary in Iran, and who was used of the Lord

to lead many Muslims to Christ) put it
like this:

> What is it that has induced Muslims
> to renounce the religion of Islam, and
> put their trust in Christ alone for salva-
> tion? It is not the similarities, but the
> great differences between the Gospel
> of Christ and the religion that has
> Mecca as its centre. It is the difference
> between faith in a loving Father in
> Heaven, who like the good shepherd
> seeks for the one who is lost till he finds
> it, and submission to the unpredictable
> will of an all-powerful God who is
> unlike anything that one can imagine,
> and is therefore unknowable; between
> putting one's trust in God's Son who
> died as a sacrifice for sinners, and
> attempting to save oneself by doing
> works of merit, which will never be
> enough to cancel one's sins; between
> following a living Lord who conquered
> death by rising from the tomb on the
> third day and is with his disciples al-
> ways, and making a pilgrimage to the
> grave of a man who died more than

1300 years ago and whose tomb is not empty; between the possibility of living a pure and holy life in the power of the Holy Spirit, and struggling in one's own strength to overcome sin and Satan and live a life pleasing to a holy God; between having as one's example and guide the sinless Son of God, and the 'Prophet' from Mecca who, according to the Qur'an, was only a man like other men, and was commanded by God to repent of his sins; between facing death with the assurance of immediate entrance into the Father's House to be forever in the holy presence of Christ, and undergoing the terrifying questioning of the two angels, and the possibility of final entrance into the fires of hell. The realisation of these and other basic differences between the two religions has caused not a few sincere seekers for God to choose the 'Pearl of Great Price', whatever the cost might be (Matt. 13:45).

(Quoted in *A Christian's Response to Islam* – Presbyterian & Reformed Pub. Co. 1976 – pages 146-147.)

Let us through love, prayer and the power of God's Spirit seek so to witness to that which is unique in the Gospel that some of our Muslim friends might also choose the 'Pearl of Great Price', whatever the cost may be.

CHAPTER 5

GETTING THE APPROACH RIGHT

We have tried to understand some of the basic teachings of Islam and have also considered some of the issues involved in presenting the Gospel. We must now try to get beyond the theory to the people. When approaching a Muslim, what is thought of that person is much more important than what is actually said. Actions and reactions speak louder than words. Motives and attitudes are all-important and in this area Christians can sometimes have more problems than others because motives can be confused and complicated.

Therefore, first of all it is necessary to think about general contact with Muslims, and secondly some general principles of approach will be mentioned that will assist us in talking to Muslims about our faith.

General Approach

1) They are human beings like us. Having spent much of this booklet talking about Islam and how to communicate the Gospel to Muslims we now, surprisingly, want to say that the most important way to achieve the right approach is to forget that the person is a Muslim and remember that he or she is a person. Let us not see them as representatives of the Islamic brotherhood or fundamentalist Islam or whatever, but as people with their own identity and good and bad points just like everyone else.

Many feel that the distinction between the Jews and Samaritans of New Testament times is similar to the distinction between Christians and Muslims today. In Jesus' day, no Jew had a good word to say about a Samaritan (see John 8:48), but Jesus himself was different. He told a story about someone who cared for a wounded traveller – the good Samaritan (Luke 10:25-37), and he healed ten lepers and the one to say thank you was a Samaritan (Luke 17:11-19). We need to be open to Muslims in the same way and appreciate them as people. Sincere Muslims have much in common with sincere Christians. They are struggling to do good and are tempted by evil. They are sometimes lonely, disappointed, troubled, sick or facing death. At the same time, we must also appreciate the Muslim who seems to have no religious concerns and shows no interest in the message of the Gospel.

2) They respond to love and friendship. This is important. Friendship is valued by people of all societies and cultures. It is never out of place. The Lord's command to his people in the Old Testament to 'love the stranger' is relevant to the Muslim today. It is not a conditional love, to be given to some if they look like responding to our message, but a genuine concern for each person whatever their background. Christian love has been the chief influence in the conversion of Muslims. Be practical in your love. Help in any way that you can without being patronising, be respectful, listen and try to understand their point of view. Remember also to be prepared to receive help from them. Being in someone's debt often helps to cement a friendship.

3) Don't be impatient. If you are building a friendship with a Muslim, don't rush to explain the Gospel. Opportunities will come through questions. Accept the fact that if your friend comes to faith it will be a long haul and you will only be one part in the chain. We are not looking for quick results!

4) Live a godly life. The character of the Christian is as important as the message told, particularly at the beginning of a Muslim's interest in Christianity. The fruit of the Spirit needs to characterise our lives: love, joy, peace, patience, kindness, goodness, faithfulness, gentleness and self-control. The last of these involves a seriousness and reverence which can sometimes be lacking in some Christian meetings. In spite of misunderstanding the way of salvation, many Muslims have a keener sense of the transcendence of God, his majesty and holiness than many Christians. A godly life demands showing respect, giving honour where it is due, being scrupulously honest in all transactions and being polite.

Christians need to live godly lives in their relationships. Many Muslims will regard Western accepted patterns of behaviour as definitely evil. A proper respect between the sexes and moderation in the demonstration of physical attraction will be a great witness by Christians.

Many Muslims see alcoholic drink as part of decadent Western society and we have to be very careful that we do not cause offence in this area.

5) Hospitality. If you enter the residence of a Muslim you will almost invariably be offered food and drink. Hospitality is a way of life in the Middle East and in Asia. The New Testament writers take up the accepted cultural norm of hospitality and emphasise it as a requirement in the Church towards both Christians and non-Christians.

Christians should also offer hospitality, and particularly in the case of Muslim students from overseas, arrange for them to visit local Christian homes where they can also be offered hospitality.

Approach in Conversation

In Acts chapter 17 from verse 16 onwards we read how the apostle Paul acted in a culture that was totally different from what he had been used to. He had met many Greeks before, of course, but here in Athens the Greek philosophy had taken over and there were probably not many places in the New Testament world where the residents' lifestyle could be described as 'spending their time doing nothing but talking about and listening to the latest ideas'. Several of the points we have to make about approach are well illustrated from these verses.

1) **Be a good listener.** Someone said once that we have two ears and only one mouth. This is well worth repeating if it encourages Christians to be good

listeners. When Paul started speaking on the Areopagus in Athens it was obvious from what he said that he had already done much listening, looking and reading.

However much you know about Islam, you will learn more by listening to Muslims. Ask questions about what they think and how they react to different situations. Don't listen to criticise, but listen to understand. When they explain something to you, try to explain what they believe back to them. Say to the person, 'I think I understand, you mean you believe that...' This approach will not only teach you much about Islam, but will show your friend that you are interested in them as a person and make them more willing to listen to you on a later occasion. Remember that not every Muslim understands their faith and many are not fully orthodox in what they believe. Listen to what they say and you may save yourself from arguing against things your friend does not in fact believe. Do not tell Muslims what they believe! Just take their word for it.

2) Never criticise Muhammad or the Qur'an. Paul could easily have attacked the ideas and writings of the Epicurean and Stoic philosophers in Athens, but instead he seemed to highlight some of their writings in order to make a point. It is unnecessary to know many details about the life and character of Muhammad as little seems to be known with absolute certainty anyway. The Qur'an is even more important to the Muslim than the person of Muhammad. Have respect for their book, although, of course, don't give the impression that you agree with all that it says.

Muhammad was a sincere man who was concerned about the idolatry around him and wanted to bring people back to the worship of the one God. We cannot criticise him, even in our thoughts, without remembering the sad fact that the Christianity he rejected was a heretical Christianity that did little to commend the Gospel. Heretical Christianity can have devastating results.

3) Start with what the person knows. Paul in Athens starts talking about an altar that the Athenians had built and goes on to talk about the possibility of knowing the 'unknown God'. When we talk to Muslims we should start where they are. Prayer is an important part of a Muslim's religious life. If the person prays regularly, ask when and why. How important is it to prostrate oneself in prayer? Why is a mat used? Do they believe God always hears them? Does God just listen to prayer or answer it?

You can talk about the character of God. The Muslim has a very high view of God. Ask about the 99 names of God and what they imply. Discuss the nature of sin and how we can be forgiven. Do we just have to ask for forgiveness?

The Muslim knows that God is light and in him there is no darkness at all. They also know that a person must be pure in order to approach God in prayer. We must build on what they already know.

4) Concentrate on Jesus. Paul concentrated on Jesus and the resurrection to such an extent that the Athenians thought that the 'resurrection' was another god to compete with Jesus. We need to be positive in our explanation of the biblical truth about Jesus.

Talk about the birth of Jesus, the character of Jesus, the stories of Jesus and the death of Jesus. Describe him as the Word of God, not the Son of God because that just introduces unhelpful misunderstandings (see Chapter 2).

Many Muslims today are very interested in the person of Jesus. He draws crowds of admirers, as he did during his life on earth, so we need to talk about him and the daily relationship we enjoy with him that affects our whole lives.

5) Avoid arguments. A discussion about a difference of belief between friends can be very helpful, but an argument where each party is simply trying to win has no value. We know of no Muslim who has ever been argued into the kingdom of God, but there are many examples of Muslims whose attitude to Christ has been hardened by argument.

6) Talk personally to Muslims alone. One of the main aims of the increased Islamic profile today is to provide a rallying point for the Muslim cause and to confirm half-hearted Muslims in the faith. If an argument does develop between Muslims and Christians, Muslims will often argue vehemently, as much to convince neighbours and friends that they are true to the cause, as to counter the Christian position. Any Muslim known to be thinking seriously about Christianity is likely to be 'rescued' by fellow Muslims.

Personal conversations with Muslims about the faith must, therefore, be on a one-to-one basis and in private. Take care not to speak to other Muslims about such a conversation. Privacy is essential.

Furthermore, it might be helpful to mention at this point, that in order to avoid any misunderstanding in your witnessing, men should be in contact with men and women with women.

A good summary of what we have been saying is found in the following statement prepared by an African Christian leader, himself a convert from Islam.

10 COMMANDMENTS
for sharing the gospel with Muslims

1. **Use the Word of God** – Muslims respect the sacred books: the Law of Moses, the Psalms, the Gospels and the Qur'an. Let the Word of God speak for itself. The Gospels are the best portions to start with, particularly Matthew and Luke.

2. **Be constantly in prayer** – It is the Holy Spirit who wins people to Christ. Seek His guidance and power as you present the Word.

3. **Be a genuine friend** – Saying 'hello' isn't enough. If you really care, show it by inviting them to your home, sharing your time and helping with their problems.

4. **Ask thought-provoking questions** – 'Do you expect to go to heaven? Do you have the assurance that God will accept you? What does the Qur'an teach about forgiveness? May I show you what the Bible teaches?' Questions like these show that you have an interest in the important things of life.

5. **Listen attentively** – When you ask a question, courtesy requires that you listen to the answer no matter how long it takes. You'll be surprised at how much you'll learn.

6. **Present your beliefs openly** – State what you believe, clearly and without apology, showing Scripture passages to support those teachings. Thus, you place the responsibility for doctrine where it belongs – on the Word of God.

7. **Reason, don't argue** – Argument may win a point but lose a hearing. There are some points on which you can argue forever without achieving a thing, except closing a mind against you.

8. **Never denigrate Muhammad or the Qur'an** – This is as offensive to them as speaking disrespectfully about Christ or the Bible is to us.

9. **Respect their customs and sensitivities** – Don't offend by putting your Bible (a holy book) on the floor, or appearing too free with the opposite sex, or refusing hospitality, or making jokes about sacred topics such as fasting, prayer or God.

10. **Persevere** – Muslims have a lot of re-thinking to do when they are confronted with the gospel. But rest assured that the Word of God will do its work in His good time.

Use of resources

In addition to talking to Muslims about your faith, it is also helpful to pass on something for them to read. This could be in English but preferably in the person's own language. An address is given in the appendix from where literature in different languages can be obtained. As pointed out in chapter two, don't hesitate to make use of the Gospel accounts ('Injil') as many enjoy reading the Scriptures in their own language for they can easily understand them, and find that it focuses on a person for whom they have great admiration and respect.

Make use of other resources such as videos, e.g. the 'Jesus' film which is now available in many different languages.

Helping New Believers

If a Muslim does choose to follow Christ we shall be called upon to give much tender loving care. Be prepared to give much personal time to encourage them in the basics of their new life in Christ. This applies particularly to their understanding of the Bible and prayer.

The Muslim idea of Scripture is different from the Christian view so the new believer from a Muslim background needs special help to know how to read the Bible. In Islam there is an emphasis on reciting the Qur'an, so we need to make it clear that Christians do not regard the Bible as a book merely to be recited. Rather, it exists in our own languages to be studied and understood. As the inspired Word of God, it is God's voice bringing God's message and therefore contains God's instructions on how we are to live as Christians. As they read they should find out what God says about how to live their everyday life. Above all, the whole Bible bears witness to Jesus Christ and so deepens our trust in God through him. So spend time reading the Bible with them and try to enrol them in a daily Bible reading scheme.

Similarly we need to explain the meaning of prayer. For as with Qur'an recitation, Muslim prayer is a ritual which must be performed exactly, and always in Arabic. Knowing the meaning of the words seems less important than the matter of performing it correctly. Therefore, we need to make it clear that the Christian does not think of prayer primarily as 'performing a ritual'. Christians think of it more as a conversation with God who is their heavenly Father, and to whom they can speak in any language they know.

We also need to explain that the essential meaning of being a Christian is not only to have a personal trust in God through Christ but also to be in fellowship with others who have a similar trust. This aspect of Christian living is of great relevance to the new believer from Islam. Most Muslims do not feel that 'being a Muslim' means primarily holding particular beliefs or doctrines but rather belonging to a certain community in which the religious, political and social links are very strong.

It is for this reason that the community is horrified if any member leaves Islam to join another religion for it is felt that the person has not made a private decision of faith but rather has become a sort of 'traitor' who has joined a rival community. Obviously, if the person is living away from their own community the immediate possibility of ostracism is lessened, but it is important for the new believer to be part of a new community with a caring, sharing fellowship of Christians whom they feel they can trust. We must be prepared to become a real family to those who do meet rejection.

Concerning witness, do not expose them to publicity or pressure that might put them on the spot with family or countrymen. Do not ask them to give their testimony in public too quickly, especially in the presence of Muslims, but prayerfully wait for them to come to the place of wanting to share their faith in this way.

So in helping the new believer we can see that the more we surround them with the truth of God's Word and the love of Christ, the more we can prepare them for all that lies ahead, whatever that might be. Let us therefore through love, prayer and the power of God's Spirit seek to build up new believers so that they will continue to follow Christ whatever the cost may be.

APPENDIX

Recommended Reading

A Christian's Pocket Guide to Islam. Patrick Sookhdeo (Christian Focus Publications 2010)

Cross and Crescent – Responding to the Challenge of Islam. Colin Chapman (IVP 2007)

Connecting with Muslims. Fouad Masri (IVP 2014)

Grace for Muslims? – The journey from fear to faith. Steve Bell (Authentic 2006)

Gospel for Muslims. Steve Bell (Authentic 2012)

I Dared to Call Him Father (testimony). Bilquis Sheikh (Chosen Books 2003)

Seeking Allah, Finding Jesus (testimony) Nabeel Qureshi (Zondervan 2014)

For evangelistic literature in English and other languages contact:

> KITAB – Interserve Resources
> Tel: 01908 552714
> Email: sales@kitab.org.uk
> Web: www.kitab.org.uk

About the Author:

Malcolm Steer lived in Iran for nine years before returning to the UK after the Revolution in 1979. Since then, for the past thirty years he has been involved in a ministry of evangelism, pastoral care and Bible teaching to Iranians in the UK and Europe.

A Christian's Pocket Guide to

Islam

Patrick Sookhdeo

REVISED
EDITION

A Christian's
Pocket Guide To Islam
Patrick Sookhdeo

This book has been written to outline the world-view, practices and history of Islam, to help non-Muslims understand their Muslim friends and neighbours better. Topics covered include the Islamic sacred books and articles of faith, the key religious observances, and the differences to be found among Muslims. The story of Islam is traced from its beginnings in the 7th century to the present. Non-Muslims who read this book will gain an understanding of why Muslims think and act as they do.

Patrick Sookhdeo is Director of the Institute for the Study of Islam and Christianity, a Christian research institute specialising in the status of Christian minorities in the Muslim world. Dr Sookhdeo is a well-known lecturer and author who holds a Ph.D. from London University's School of Oriental and African Studies and a D.D. from Western Seminary, Oregon, USA.

ISBN 978-1-84550-572-1

Christian Focus Publications

Our mission statement –

STAYING FAITHFUL

In dependence upon God we seek to impact the world through literature faithful to His infallible Word, the Bible. Our aim is to ensure that the Lord Jesus Christ is presented as the only hope to obtain forgiveness of sin, live a useful life and look forward to heaven with Him.

Our Books are published in four imprints:

CHRISTIAN
FOCUS

Popular works including biographies, commentaries, basic doctrine and Christian living.

CHRISTIAN
HERITAGE

Books representing some of the best material from the rich heritage of the church.

MENTOR

Books written at a level suitable for Bible College and seminary students, pastors, and other serious readers. The imprint includes commentaries, doctrinal studies, examination of current issues and church history.

CF4•K

Children's books for quality Bible teaching and for all age groups: Sunday school curriculum, puzzle and activity books; personal and family devotional titles, biographies and inspirational stories – Because you are never too young to know Jesus!

Christian Focus Publications Ltd,
Geanies House, Fearn, Ross-shire,
IV20 1TW, Scotland, United Kingdom.
www.christianfocus.com